LINKING THE PAST AND PRESENT

WHAT DID THE
ANCIENT
CHINESE
DO FOR ME?

Patrick Catel

Heinemann Library
Chicago, Illinois

Printed and bound in China by CTPS

14 13 12 11 10
10 9 8 7 6 5 4 3 2

Library of Congress Cataloging-in-Publication Data
Catel, Patrick.

What did the ancient Chinese do for me? / Patrick Catel.

p. cm. -- (Linking the past and present)

Includes bibliographical references and index.

ISBN 978-1-4329-3747-8 (hc) -- ISBN 978-1-4329-3754-6
(pb)

1. China--Civilization--Juvenile literature. 2. Civilization,
Modern--Ancient influences--Juvenile literature. I. Title.

DS721.C38 2011

931--dc22

2009040022

Acknowledgments
The author and publishers are grateful to the following
for permission to reproduce copyright material: Alamy
Images p. **17** (©View Stock); The Bridgeman Art Library
p. **26** (Bibliotheque Nationale, Paris, France); Corbis pp. **7**
(Redlink/ Li Shao Bai), **15** (Louie Psihoyos), **19** (Reuters/
Vasily Fedosenko), **27** (Mike McQueen); Getty Images p. **23**
(Digital Vision); Photolibrary pp. **13** (View Stock), **21** (Chuck
Mason); Rex Features pp. **9** (Robert Harding/ Michael Snell),
11 (Robert Hallam); shutterstock p. **25** (©Bork).

Cover photograph of Great Wall of China at Simatai
reproduced with permission of istockphoto/©Jarno Gonzalez
Zarraonandia.

We would like to thank May-Lee Chai for her invaluable help
in the preparation of this book.

Every effort has been made to contact copyright holders of
any material reproduced in this book. Any omissions will
be rectified in subsequent printings if notice is given to the
publisher.

All the Internet addresses (URLs) given in this book were valid
at the time of going to press. However, due to the dynamic
nature of the Internet, some addresses may have changed, or
sites may have changed or ceased to exist since publication.
While the author and Publishers regret any inconvenience this
may cause readers, no responsibility for any such changes can
be accepted by either the author or the Publishers.

Contents

Look for the Then and Now boxes. They highlight parts of ancient Chinese culture that are present in our modern world.

Any words appearing in the text in bold, **like this**, are explained in the glossary.

What Did the Ancient Chinese Do For Me?

Our modern society owes a lot to the ancient Chinese. Have you ever enjoyed flying a kite? Playing with dominoes? Remember that time you were thankful that you had an umbrella when it started to rain? Do you practice martial arts? You probably remember eating some delicious ice cream! The ancient Chinese are to thank for all of those inventions, and many more.

The ancient Chinese invented the kite, dominoes, the folding umbrella, paper, and ice cream. They also invented the fine art of making silk, which was kept secret for hundreds of years. The ancient Chinese created a postal service, as well as matches, gunpowder, and fireworks. They even invented a **seismograph** to detect earthquakes. These are just a few of the inventions and technology of the ancient Chinese.

The ancient Chinese used gunpowder to launch **multistage rockets**.

The inventions that advanced ancient Chinese culture continue to influence our daily lives and the modern world. Look at the illustration below. Can you see some of the technology the ancient Chinese used that we still use today?

Ancient Chinese dynasties

Chinese civilization grew along with **agriculture**. Although ancient China included a huge area of land, most people settled in places that were ideal for farming. This was usually along river valleys and areas where water and good soil were easily available. Living along the rivers also allowed people to easily move and transport goods among settlements.

Ancient China was ruled by several different dynasties. A **dynasty** is when leader after leader comes to rule from the same powerful family or group. In 221 BCE, the Qin (pronounced "chin") dynasty began with the first emperor, Qin Shihuangdi. The Qin defeated six other states to create an **empire** and unite a huge area in Asia.

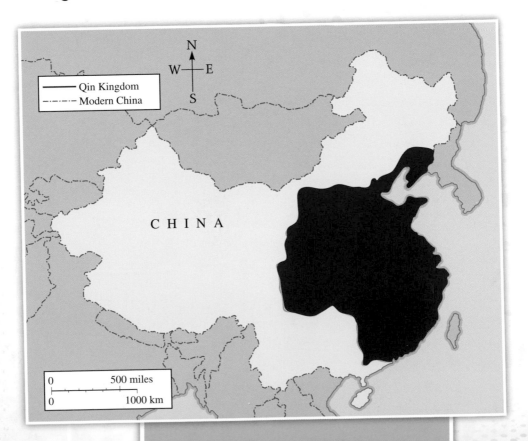

This map shows the area of land ruled by the Qin dynasty.

Two of the world's most famous historic places were built in the time of Qin Shihuangdi, who ruled from 221 BCE until his death in 210 BCE. The first place is the first emperor's **mausoleum**. It contains around 8,000 life-size warriors made from clay. The second is the Great Wall of China, which was improved and made bigger by the emperor.

Naming China

The name China comes from the Qin dynasty (221–206 BCE).

The Great Wall of China is the longest man-made structure in the world.

Ancient China was ruled by other dynasties, as you will see from the timeline on pages 28 and 29. The Han dynasty came after the Qin and lasted over 400 years, from 206 BCE to 220 CE, with a short break. The ideas that came about during the Han dynasty affected China for the next 2,000 years. Ancient China is also known for many things besides the sites of the first emperor. These include famous inventions, ideas, and philosophies that are still popular today.

What Was Daily Life Like in Ancient China?

Like many people in modern societies, the ancient Chinese were concerned about how they looked. Chinese men usually wore hats. These hats were often made of fine silk. Women in cities had mirrors, jewelry, and makeup. They used tweezers to pluck their eyebrows. Women would put crushed pearl powder on their faces to make their skin appear paler and smoother. Pearl powder is still sold today as a makeup and facial cream.

The ancient Chinese found creative and fun ways to spend their spare time, much like we do today. They used playing cards and dominoes. They also invented board games such as Go, which was similar to Othello, and Xiangqi, which was their version of chess. They had sports similar to modern sports—wrestling, archery contests, and boat races. Gymnastics was popular, and there were many competitions held around ancient China.

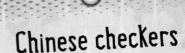

Chinese checkers

Chinese checkers is not a Chinese game. It has no relation to either China or checkers.

THEN...

The fame of ancient Chinese silk gave the trade route between China, the Middle East, and Europe the name "Silk Road." Silk is strong, soft, and easily colored and painted. The ancient Chinese traded their silk fabrics as far west as ancient Rome, where wealthy people purchased them. The skills for harvesting silk and making silk fabrics were closely guarded secrets. No one outside of China knew how it was done.

生产用蚕 请勿带走
Don't take aw... cocoons.

The art of making silk is still carried on in this modern-day factory in China. This woman is working with the cocoons of silk worms.

...NOW

The secret is out now! Silk is made from strands of the silk worm's cocoon. The silk worm is raised on a diet of mulberry leaves. It spins its cocoon after four to five weeks. The cocoon's fibers are then woven into silk. Silk is still a very popular fabric today, and China is still the world's leading producer of silk.

Food and drink

Most people around the world have experienced Chinese food. But you may not have thought of ancient China the last time you ate ice cream, even though the ancient Chinese are said to have invented the treat! Tea was an even more important food item in ancient Chinese culture. In fact, tea is mentioned in Chinese writing dating back 5,000 years. Tea has been the national drink of China throughout its history. Today, Chinese teas are popular worldwide.

Umbrellas and kites

The ancient Chinese created and used other amazing things in their daily lives, including the pottery wheel, wallpaper, porcelain china, and paper money. They even invented folding umbrellas over 3,000 years ago! Like today, there was entertainment, including music, acrobatic, and other performances. The ancient Chinese also invented the kite. They created huge kites shaped like dragons and other animals, which took great skill to fly.

Food seasoning

Adding seasoning to food once it had been served was considered rude in ancient China.

THEN...

More than 3,000 years ago, the ancient Chinese mixed snow and ice with sweet juices made from fruit and honey to create the world's first ice cream. Ice cream later spread west to Europe. It is said that when he returned from exploring China in 1295 CE, the Italian traveler Marco Polo brought back a recipe for ice cream.

Large dragon kites such as this were sometimes used in ancient China to scare or distract enemies during battles. Today, people create them as works of art and fly them for fun.

...NOW

Once the idea of ice cream was out, and people got a taste, it spread around the world. When the refrigerator and freezer were invented in the 1800s, it was even easier to make ice cream available to more people. Today ice cream is more popular than ever. Over one billion gallons of ice cream and frozen desserts are produced each year in the United States alone!

How Did the Ancient Chinese Communicate?

The ancient Chinese understood the importance of education as we do today. The Han **dynasty** created public schools, where boys learned reading, writing, math, philosophy, literature, and art. When learning math, students used an **abacus** to count. The wealthiest families hired private tutors to teach their children. Unlike today, the only way girls received an education in ancient China was if their parents were willing to hire tutors or teach them on their own.

Bad luck

The Chinese believe you should never point at anyone with chopsticks, and that putting them down in a crossed position could bring bad luck.

In the Chinese language, each character stands for a word instead of a letter. Ancient Chinese writing was a fine art known as **calligraphy**. Calligraphy artists used brushes and a mix of **lampblack** and glue was used for **ink sticks**. The artist would then add water and grind an **inkstone** against the ink stick to make liquid ink. Calligraphy is still considered very important in China, and it is practiced using many of the same ancient tools.

THEN...

The ancient Chinese created a **network** of **couriers** on horseback as a quick and reliable way of delivering messages across the **empire**. Inns along all of the main roads were used as post offices and places for the couriers to rest or pick up a fresh horse. Similar to today, the ancient Chinese even had different classes of mail.

The abacus is still used as a counting tool in many parts of Asia.

People rely on mail, communications, and shipping that operate 24 hours a day around the globe. Like in ancient China, people can pay more or less depending on what service they would like, but the options are even greater. With modern boats, planes, trains, and automobiles, letters and packages can be sent halfway around the world in less time than ever before. Many shipping companies even offer overnight delivery to most places!

Paper and printing

The ancient Chinese couldn't practice their beautiful **calligraphy** and art without paper. Using plant materials, they invented paper similar to what we use today. The ancient Chinese used this paper to keep written records that were important for running a large **empire**. Modern governments around the world rely on written records. Our modern society may not have been possible without the invention of paper.

The ancient Chinese also created block printing. In block printing, the characters for a page would be carved into wood. Ink would then be added to the wood block, which could then quickly stamp a copy of the page onto a sheet of paper. This was an early form of printing, which made cheaper, easier copies. Before the invention of block printing, writing had to be copied by hand.

Papermaking in ancient China was done by hand and took a great deal of time.

THEN...

The name "paper" comes from the word *papyrus*. This is what the ancient Egyptians used as paper. However, it was the ancient Chinese who invented paper similar to the paper we use today. In 105 CE, during the Han **dynasty**, a man named Cai Lun reported a new kind of paper to the emperor. He first used tree bark and then added plant material, old rags, and fishnets.

Printing press machines at modern paper mills, such as this one, can make thousands of printed pages in a day.

...NOW

The ideas and techniques for making paper slowly spread around the world. Many people think paper is one of the most important inventions in human history. The cheap production of thin paper allowed it to be bound in books. Paper, printing, and books helped knowledge to spread to more and more people. Societies became more educated because of paper. You wouldn't be able to read these amazing things about ancient China without paper and printing!

What Did the Ancient Chinese Do For Science?

The ancient Chinese contributed a lot to modern science and technology. They invented a **magnetic compass**, which is an important **navigation** tool still used around the world. They also invented **cast iron** and the ship rudder (used to steer ships). The ship rudder was an important development for sea travel. China has always suffered from earthquakes. As early as 132 CE, during the Han **dynasty**, the Chinese invented the first **seismograph** to detect them!

Astronomy

The ancient Chinese practiced astronomy. Zhang Heng, the inventor of the seismograph, was a well-known astronomer in ancient China. The ancient Chinese created some of the first records of important events in the sky. They carefully studied the movements of the Sun and Moon, in order to create accurate calendars. Accurate calendars were needed to predict the seasons and have success in farming, which would provide enough food for people.

THEN...

The ancient Chinese seismograph looked like a large urn, or jar, and was made of copper. On the outside were eight dragons, facing down and placed in opposite directions, with a toad below each one. Each dragon held a bronze ball in its mouth. A tremor in the earth would cause the urn to lose balance. The ball would drop from one of the dragon's mouths into the toad below and make a sound. People would then know the time and direction of the earthquake, and officials could send help in the right direction.

This ancient Chinese seismograph helped people know when an earthquake struck. It was decorated with dragons because the Chinese believed that most dragons were good and served as protectors.

...NOW

Not only did the Chinese invent a seismograph so long ago, they also understood how to make buildings resistant to the shocks of earthquakes. Most structures were made from wood. The connecting joints of beams and columns were built to be flexible, in order to absorb vibrations. Seismographs have advanced through the years, and measurements of earthquakes are more precise. There are many people living in earthquake zones in China and around the world, and earthquake detection and construction ideas are more important than ever before.

Matches

Next time you see someone use a match, thank the ancient Chinese for that invention. They coated little sticks of pinewood with **sulfur**, which would easily burst into flame. And of course, the ancient Chinese are famous for their invention of gunpowder. With their knowledge of fire and the chemicals of gunpowder, the ancient Chinese invented fireworks. Even more impressive, however, is that the ancient Chinese invented **multistage rockets**.

The Chinese invented multistage rockets, such as this one, hundreds of years before they would be used to take humans to the Moon.

THEN...

One ancient Chinese multistage rocket was designed to look like a dragon. There were four rockets on the outside, which were the first-stage rockets. The inside of the tube was also filled with rockets. These were the second-stage rockets, which would ignite automatically once the first-stage rockets were done. They would then come out of the dragon's mouth at the front end of the tube and shoot toward the enemy.

The art of war

The ancient Chinese were often at war, so they invented things to be used in warfare. One of these inventions was the crossbow. Even after early guns were invented, the crossbow was still more accurate and quicker to reload. The ancient Chinese created a flame-thrower, made with brass parts, that could be used in warfare. Using a pump action, it could shoot out a continuous stream of flame.

Scaring the enemy
The ancient Chinese army sometimes used kites in the shapes of monsters to frighten enemies.

The fireworks we enjoy on special occasions would not be possible without the ancient Chinese invention of gunpowder.

...NOW

With their inventions of gunpowder and the multistage rocket, the ancient Chinese took the first steps that eventually led human beings to visit space and the Moon. Multistage rockets have allowed space exploration. When one stage of lift-off is done, the first rocket detaches. This makes the rocket lighter when the second-stage rocket ignites, and so on.

How Did the Ancient Chinese Grow Crops?

Ancient Chinese knowledge of **agriculture** allowed them to feed more people more easily, which then allowed more people to live in smaller areas. The ancient Chinese created several inventions to help their farming, including the animal harness and iron plow. The iron plow used by the ancient Chinese was stronger and more advanced than any other tool in the world at the time. It could even be adjusted to plow at different depths in the soil.

Planting crops in rows

The iron plow would not be found in Europe until more than 1,000 years later. The ancient Chinese idea of planting crops in rows was probably as important as the iron plow, because crops grow more quickly this way. **Irrigation**, or the watering of crops, is easier when crops are planted in rows. The Chinese iron plows, driven by harnessed animals, were also easier to use when the crops were planted in rows.

Growing rice

In some areas of China, fields are flooded so rows of rice seedlings can grow. These fields are called "paddies."

THEN...

Only a small part of the land of ancient China was useful for farming. As the population grew, the ancient Chinese had to find better ways to feed people. They learned to make hilly land level, began planting crops in rows, and used their iron plows for furrowing. Furrowing is when ditches, or furrows, are cut in between the rows of planted crops. These furrows then hold water. This is called furrow irrigation.

Modern farms rely on machines to make the job easier and produce more food, faster. However, crops are still planted in rows, just as they first were in ancient China.

...NOW

The ancient Chinese advances and ideas in agriculture are still used in farming today. The world is more populated than it has ever been, and farming has to be efficient in order to produce enough food for everyone. Crops are still planted in rows, much as in ancient China. Even the metal plow hasn't changed much, although now it is usually made of steel and often powered by a large, modern engine.

Winnowing

The ancient Chinese invented other tools to make farming and work easier and more productive. Winnowing is the separating of husks and stalks, also known as chaff, from the grains after they have been harvested. In the past, the way people did this was to simply throw the mixture in the air. The wind blows away the lighter chaff, but the heavier grains fall down and can be gathered.

In ancient China, the wheelbarrow was called the Wooden Ox or the Gliding Horse. It was used to transport rice, vegetables, and even people!

THEN...

The ancient Chinese invented some amazing and complex things. However, one Chinese invention that was very simple is still used today, with very little change: the wheelbarrow. There is evidence that the wheelbarrow may have been invented during the Han **dynasty** (206 BCE–220 CE). It allowed Chinese farmers to more easily carry heavier weights from place to place.

Rotary winnowing fan

The ancient Chinese invented the rotary winnowing fan to make the process of separating the grain from the chaff easier. With the rotary winnowing fan, there was a crank attached that could be turned to power a fan. The fan would then create an air stream used to separate the grain from the chaff. The chaff was blown off, and the grains fell straight down into a basket. Similar machines are still used around the world today.

Today, people all around the world make use of the wheelbarrow. It has changed very little in 2,000 years.

...NOW

The wheelbarrow is a simple device, but very effective. Its one wheel makes it easier to maneuver on rough land. It also makes it easier for a person to control where the contents go when dumped out. The wheelbarrow was such an ingenious invention that it is still used around the world, and has changed little over time. Wheelbarrows can be found at most farms, construction sites, and even many homes today.

What Type of Medicine Was Practiced in Ancient China?

Ancient Chinese doctors practiced what is today called **traditional** Chinese medicine. They created medical guides and even an encyclopedia of medical knowledge by the time of the Han **dynasty** (206 BCE–220 CE). The ancient Chinese believed in what is called **holistic** medicine. This means they would not only treat an illness, but would also treat the problem that caused the illness. They believed problems were caused by an imbalance of energy, or **qi** (pronounced "chee"), in a person's body.

Ancient exams and treatments

A Chinese doctor would give a person a thorough exam, asking questions about the person's symptoms and history. The doctor would listen to the person's breathing, check for strange odors, and check the person's pulse. Treatments included special diets, **herbal remedies**, exercises, and acupuncture. These treatments were meant to restore balance and health. Traditional Chinese medicine is still practiced today and has become popular outside of China.

THEN...

Ancient Chinese medicine included herbal remedies such as **ginseng**, which is still popular today. It also included acupuncture, which is a method of placing thin needles into specific points of the body where the Chinese believed energy flowed. If done properly, it should cause no pain, and should actually relieve pain. Acupuncture was meant to restore the balanced flow of energy in the body. It was used to help treat many kinds of injury and disease.

It may seem very strange that putting pins in the body could help it heal, but recent evidence shows that it can work. Today, people around the world use acupuncture to treat illness and relieve pain.

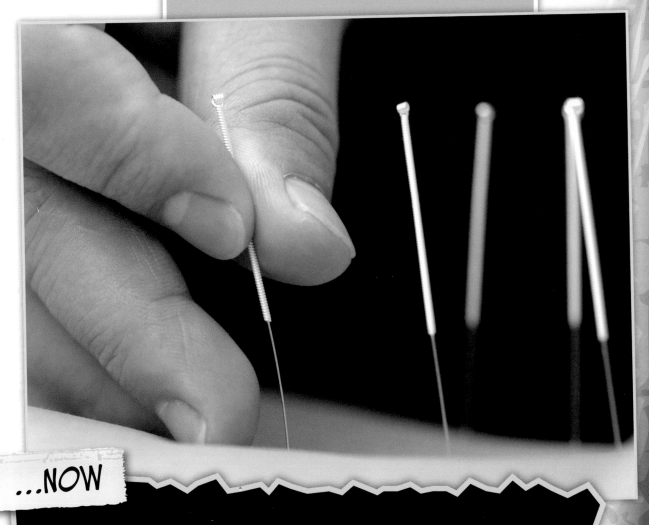

...NOW

Today in China, doctors practice both modern medicine and the traditional methods of their history. This combination of traditional and modern medicine is now popular outside of China as well. Acupuncture has become popular as scientific studies have shown that it really works for many kinds of pain and illness. There are now clinics around the world that teach students to practice traditional Chinese acupuncture.

Chinese beliefs

Ancient Chinese beliefs and philosophies played an important role in the development of Chinese culture. Two main systems of belief came from ancient China. These were Confucianism and Daoism. Confucianism is named after Confucius, who was a wandering scholar in ancient China in the 400s BCE. Confucianism emphasizes education and teaches order and harmony in life and government.

Confucius (right) was one of the first people to express "the Golden Rule." He said, "Do not to others what you do not want done to yourself."

THEN...

Ancient Chinese philosophy and medicine reflect the Chinese ideas of balance. If things are in balance, with equal parts yin and yang, there will be good physical and spiritual health. Daoists (followers of Daoism) believed that both the mind and body must be exercised to promote spiritual health. To do this, they created exercises for the body that would help balance the flow of qi, or energy, in the body.

Daoism (pronounced "dow-ism") was the other major belief system in ancient China. Confucianism is more concerned with day-to-day rules of conduct. Daoism is concerned with a more spiritual and natural way of living. The word *dao* means "the way." Daoism is thought to have come from a man named Laozi (pronounced "Lau dzih"). He lived around the same time as Confucius. Daoism has now become a religion.

Tai Chi is also considered a martial art. It probably inspired other martial arts, such as Kung Fu, which also developed in ancient China.

...NOW

Today, the Dao De Jing has been translated more frequently than any work except the Bible, and its wise sayings are often quoted. Many people around the world also practice the physical exercises inspired by Daoism, called Tai Chi. Tai Chi consists of slow, graceful movements that flow from one to the next. Practitioners are supposed to clear their minds and focus on their breathing and flowing energy, or qi.

Key Dates

Here is an outline of important dates in ancient Chinese history and when important inventions and developments in ancient Chinese culture were made:

around 500 BCE	**Cast iron** is developed in China
400s BCE	Confucianism and Daoism are developed as belief systems
	Kites are in use
221 BCE	Qin Shihuangdi becomes China's first emperor. He founds the Qin **dynasty**, which defeats other states to create an **empire**.
221–206 BCE	**Irrigation** projects, roads, and canals are built
	Qin Shihuangdi orders a huge building project to extend the Great Wall of China
	Qin Shihuangdi's mausoleum and terracotta warriors are built
206 BCE	The Han dynasty begins
1st century BCE	Development of the Silk Road
1st century CE	An early type of **magnetic compass** is developed
around 105 CE	Paper is invented
around 120 CE	Cast iron plows and other tools are in widespread use

132 CE	Earliest evidence of **seismographs** in use
around 200 CE	The wheelbarrow is in use
	Ship's rudder in use
220 CE	The Han dynasty ends
220–280 CE	During this period tea is in use, **calligraphy** is popular, and there is a growth in the popularity of Daoism
400s CE	Umbrellas are in use
around 600s CE	Porcelain pottery is developed
	Block printing is in use
	Matches are in use
around 900 CE	Gunpowder is in use
960–1279 CE	**Multistage rockets** are developed

Glossary

abacus counting device that is a frame holding a row of rods with movable counters

agriculture farming crops and raising livestock

BCE short for "before Christian era." BCE is used for all the years before year 1.

calligraphy art of beautiful writing

cast iron hard mixture of iron, carbon, and other elements that can be cast into different shapes

courier messenger carrying messages or packages with speed

dynasty when leader after leader comes to rule from the same powerful family or group

empire group of nations or peoples ruled over by a powerful leader or government

ginseng plant that is supposed to have health benefits

herbal remedy plant materials used to prevent, treat, or cure illness

holistic paying attention to and treating the problem that caused an illness as well as treating the illness itself

ink stick mix of lampblack and glue formed into a stick

inkstone slab of stone used to grind an ink stick

irrigation supplying land with water to assist in growing crops

lampblack fine, black soot

magnetic compass compass with a magnetized needle that points to Earth's magnetic poles

mausoleum large, stately tomb

multistage rocket rocket that has two or more parts that fire one after another

navigation plotting and directing the course of a journey

network complex, connected group or system

qi (pronounced "chee," and sometimes spelled "chi"). Chinese word for the energy and breath in the body

seismograph machine that measures the shaking of the ground

sulfur common yellow chemical that burns with a strong smell

traditional handed down by tradition, which is the usual and established practice

Find Out More

Books

Doeden, Matt. The Chinese: Life in China's Golden Age
(Life in Ancient Civilizations). Minneapolis, MN:
Millbrook Press, 2009.

Friedman, Mel. Ancient China (True Books). New York:
Scholastic, 2009.

Guillain, Charlotte. Ancient China (China Focus).
Chicago: Heinemann Library, 2009.

Shuter, Jane. Ancient China (Time Travel Guides).
Chicago: Raintree, 2007.

Snedden, Robert. Ancient China (Technology in Times Past).
Collingwood, ON: Saunders, 2009.

Websites

http://www.historyforkids.org/learn/china/
This site, run by Kidipede, provides all kinds of links discussing
different features of ancient Chinese culture, history, and science.

http://www.ancientchina.co.uk/menu.html
This site, run by the British Museum, discusses various features
of ancient Chinese civilization.

http://www.wsu.edu/~dee/ANCCHINA/ANCCHINA.HTM
This web page offers links to lots more information about
ancient Chinese civilization.

Index